Welcome

Cont

Catch on
to a
sensation

x

ents

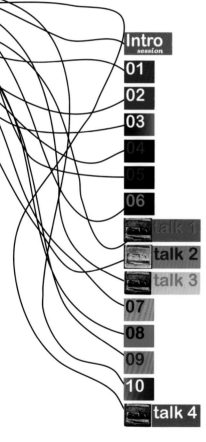

Christianity

DIRECTION FOR A LOST WORLD 1

REALITY IN A CONFUSED WORLD 2

LIFE IN A DARK WORLD 3

Intro session

Where are you headed?
Not right now, not this moment, this week, this year or even this decade ...
Let's talk about the ultimate goal of your life, and even about what happens after death.

Jesus said, 'I am the way.'

With Jesus to show us the way we can have a life full of purpose and meaning – and fun.

It's a crazy, mixed-up world we live in. People are confused and many don't even know it.
But what you believe matters. It determines the course of your life.

Jesus said, 'I am the truth.'

With Jesus to show us the truth we can make sense of the world around us.

It's dark out there. The world can be a dark place and the line between darkness and light passes through the heart of each of us. Every human has the potential to do good or to do evil with their lives.

Jesus said, 'I am the life.'

With Jesus we can turn our backs on evil, on the dark side, and live forever in the light.

EXTRA

Today it is popular to argue that it doesn't matter what you believe so long as you are sincere. But surely, that is crazy? Nothing matters so much as what we believe. Hitler's sincere beliefs led to the deaths of millions of Jews. Jack the Ripper's sincere beliefs led him to murder prostitutes. More positively, Nelson Mandela's sincere beliefs drove him to lead his people to freedom. What you believe matters; it determines the course of your life. Nowhere is that more true than in the arena of faith. The brilliant academic and Christian writer C. S. Lewis put it this way, 'Christianity is a statement which, if false, is of no importance, and, if true, of infinite importance. The one thing it cannot be is moderately important.'
Do yourself a favour: take the time to examine your beliefs.

Jesus said, 'I am the way, the truth and the life'
John 14:6

Boring,
Untrue,
Irrelevant

?

can't get no satisfaction.'

Mick Jagger

e're just wandering
ound waiting to
e...bumping into
ch other and
chieving a few things.'

Chris Evans

fe is like a broken pencil...pointless!'

Introduction

'm young and this is the start of the 21ST Century!
What on earth does Christianity have to offer me?

Primary Sources

'I came so they can have
real and eternal life,
more and better life than
they ever dreamed of.'

**Jesus of Nazareth (John
10:10 THE MESSAGE)**

lusion

anity is not boring – it is about living life to the full.
anity is not untrue – it is *the* truth.
nity is not irrelevant – it transforms the whole of our lives

Who Jesus

'The only Jesus for whom we have any evidence at all is a gigantic figure making stupendous claims.'

✳ **Archbishop Temple**

Introduction

Different people have different ideas about who Jesus was We do know that Jesus existed and most people agree these facts about him: Jewish man who was born in Bethlehem in Judaea around 4 BC Famous as a great teacher and miracle worker Crucified by the Roman authorities. His followers believed he was the Son of God and that he rose from the dead, and they took the good news through the world. The New Testament of the Bible is our best source of information about Jesus.

Primary Sources

'You don't have to wait for the end. I am, right now, Resurrection and Life. The one who believes in me, even though he or she dies, will live. And everyone who lives believing in me does not ultimately die at all. Do you believe this?'

✳ **(JOHN 11:26-27 THE MESSAGE)**

01

Very few people could have as magnetic a personality as Christ, and no actor has got that. You will always know you are looking at an actor pretending to be someone infinitely greater than he is ... the whole point about Christ, if you believe in Christ, is that Christ is divine, not that he was a jolly good chap.

❋ Barry Norman, talking about films portraying Christ

JESUS WAS FULLY HUMAN
John 4:6

He had a body, emotions and experiences just like ours. The question that we must ask is, 'Was he more than human? Was he God?'

WHAT DID HE SAY ABOUT HIMSELF
John 11:25-26

This wise teacher also made outrageous claims about himself:

I am the bread of life

I am the light of the world

I am the resurrection and the life

I am the way and the truth and the life

He claimed to be able to forgive sins

He claimed to be the one who would judge the world

He claimed to be the Messiah

He claimed to be Son of God

He claimed to be God the Son Jesus didn't make it possible for us to think of him as just a good man. A normal man who said the things Jesus said wouldn't be a good man at all. If he believed what he said he would have to be a mad man. If he didn't believe it but said it anyway (just to get influence over people) then he would be a bad man, a con man. So, why do we believe that Jesus was not a mad man or a con man but the one and only God man?

01

WHAT EVIDENCE IS THERE?

Matthew 5-7

- His teaching
- His works
- His character
- His fulfilment of Old Testament prophecy
- His resurrection from the dead

'All the armies that ever marched, and all the navies that ever sailed, and all the parliaments that ever sat, and all the kings that ever reigned, put together have not affected the life of humans on earth as has that one solitary life.'

Anonymous

REAL LIFE STORIES

BENNY Murphy

Medicine Student, Edinburgh University

Who Is J

I come from a Christian background, but I come from a little village in Dorset where the vast majority of the church are over 60. I'd heard about the Alpha course before coming to university, but I heard more at the Freshers' Fair. I was quite interested and signed up. On the first night, it was really nice coming into a friendly atmosphere – and I just kept coming. I'd always thought of Jesus as a kind of fairy-tale myth – not as a real person – but during the first few weeks of the course, I saw all the evidence for his having lived. It really brought it home to me. It was amazing. The people in my group had quite different backgrounds and there were many different perspectives, which was really useful. Jesus has made a real difference in my life. It is just knowing that there is someone who totally accepts me and who has created me. It has helped to understand people more and to understand their needs ✷

work	when written	earliest copy	time lapse	no. of copies
Herodotus	488-428 BC	AD 900	1,300 years	8
Thucydides	c.460-100 BC	c.AD 900	1,300 years	8
Tacitus	AD 100	AD 1100	1,000 years	20
Caesar's Gallic War	58-50 BC	AD 900	950 years	9-10
Livy's Roman History	59 BC-AD 17	AD 900	900 years	20
New Testament	AD 40-100	AD 130 (manuscripts AD 350)	30-310 years	5,000 +Greek 10,000 Latin 9,300 others

show me the evidence

Christianity is not some ephemeral, willow-the-wisp whimsy invented by a bored mystic or philosopher. Christianity is an historical faith – based on actual events that took place in time and space. Christianity is based upon historical fact.

This is what one of the 'history men' of the time (not a Christian but a Jew) had to say about Jesus:

'Now there was about this time, a wise man, if it be lawful to call him a man, for he was a doer of wonderful works – a teacher of such men who receive the truth with pleasure. He drew over to him both many of the Jews, and many of the Gentiles. He was [the] Christ; and when Pilate, at the suggestion of the principal men amongst us, had condemned him to the cross, those that loved him at first did not forsake him, for he appeared to them alive again the third day, as the divine prophets had foretold these and ten thousand other wonderful things concerning him; and the tribe of Christians so named after him, are not extinct at this day.' Josephus

Of course, Jesus was just a peripheral character in the writings of the Jewish and Roman historians. To really get into Jesus' life we turn to the New Testament of the Christian Bible. Before you start crying 'Foul!' let's go on a flying tour of a science known as textual criticism.

Textual criticism shows that the charge that the New Testament as we have it today is different to what was originally written is unfounded. Check out this table to see how much better documented the New Testament is than any other ancient text ...

Conclusion
Fashions, fads and crazes come and go, but 2000 years after the death of Jesus not millions, but billions of people follow him.

Why Did Jesus Die

Introduction ‹‹‹‹‹ ‹

Why is it that an instrument of torture and execution is the most common and recognisable symbol of the Christian faith? Why is the cross at the heart of the Christian faith? * **I Corinthians 2:2**

THE PROBLEM

Romans 3:23

We humans have a problem – we have all done wrong. The Bible, and Christians who follow the Bible, call this sin.

Sin has unwanted results:
Sin pollutes us and makes us unclean
Sin's power over us grows and grows
Sin has a penalty, a punishment
Sin separates us from God

THE SOLUTION

1 Peter 2:24

God loved us so much that he took our place, substituted himself for us, and suffered the results of our sin.
Jesus' death on the cross took care of the results of sin once and for all.

THE RESULT

Romans 3:21-26

In the Bible there are different images used to explain the result of Jesus' death on the cross ... The image of:

The Temple – Pollution of sin is removed
The Market Place – Power of sin is broken
The Law Court – Penalty of sin is paid
The Home – Separation caused by sin is destroyed and we can know God

CRU...

The writer Cicero described crucifixion as 'the most cruel and hideous of tortures'. Jesus was stripped and tied to a whipping post. He was flogged with four or five thongs of leather interwoven with sharp jagged bone and lead. Eusebius, the third-century church historian, described Roman flogging in these terms: the sufferer's 'veins were laid bare, and ... the very muscles, sinews and bowels of the victim were open to exposure'. He was then taken to the

FI**X**ION

Praetorium where a crown of thorns was thrust upon his head. He was mocked by a battalion of 600 men and hit about the face and head. He was then forced to carry a heavy cross bar on his bleeding shoulders until he collapsed, and Simon of Cyrene was press-ganged into carrying it for him.

When they reached the site of crucifixion, he was again stripped naked. He was laid on the cross, and six-inch nails were driven into his forearms, just above the wrist. His knees were twisted sideways so that the ankles could be nailed between the tibia and the Achilles' tendon. He was then lifted up on the cross which was then dropped into a socket in the ground. There he was left to hang in intense heat and unbearable thirst, exposed to the ridicule of the crowd. He hung there in unthinkable pain for six hours while his life slowly drained away.

Yet the worst part of his suffering was not the physical trauma of torture and crucifixion nor even the emotional pain of being rejected by the world and deserted by his friends, but the spiritual agony of being cut off from his father for us – as he carried our sins ☀

'"There cannot be a God of love," men say, "because if there was, and he looked down upon this world, his heart would break." The church points to the cross and says, "It did break."' ___ Archbishop William Temple

Primary Sources

'But in our time something new has been added. What Moses and the prophets witnessed to all those years has happened. The God-setting-things-right that we read about has become Jesus-setting-things-right for us. And not only for us, but for everyone who believes in him. For there is no difference between us and them in this. Since we've compiled this long and sorry record as sinners (both us and them) and proved that we are utterly incapable of living the glorious lives God wills for us, God did it for us. Out of sheer generosity he put us in right standing with himself. A pure gift. He got us out of the mess we're in and restored us to where he always wanted us to be. And he did it by means of Jesus Christ.God sacrificed Jesus on the altar of the world to clear that world of sin. Having faith in him sets us in the clear. God decided on this course of action in full view of the public - to set the world in the clear with himself through the sacrifice of Jesus, finally taking care of the sins he had so patiently endured. This is not only clear, but it's now - this is current history. God sets things right. He also makes it possible for us to live in his rightness.'

✳ (Romans 3:21-26 THE MESSAGE)

REAL LIFE STORIES

OLIVER Douglas-Pennant
Psychology Student, Edinburgh University

During my first year, I did ordinary first-year things like going out and getting drunk. I wasn't interested in going to church remotely. I just didn't believe there was a God.

In my second year I moved into a flat and one of the other people in the flat, Amy, was a Christian.

I began to get some Christian friends and go to church a bit, although I still had no belief whatsoever.

Then Amy ran an Alpha course in our home and I helped her a bit, but I wasn't really interested. After that, she started running the course in the Blind Poet Pub and she asked if I would help.

I went along and helped set it up each week and took a small part in the discussions. That made me think about it a bit more deeply. I began slowly to think that maybe it really was true. I didn't have any faith at all but I just began to think, 'These people seem to have something and what they are saying is beginning to make sense.'

On one of the later weeks, we were led in a prayer at the end of the talk. I said to God I was sorry – something I'd never thought I needed to say to anyone before. That was a big step.

Jesus has made a complete difference in my life. From not having any kind of aim or reason, now I really feel that everything I am doing I want it to be for Jesus' ✳

Conclusion

Galatians 2:20

God has made a way for the results of our sin to be dealt with and for us to enter into relationship with him.

If we believe that Jesus suffered on the cross for us and if we say sorry for the things that we have done wrong (our sins) we can begin to know God.

'Life is an unanswered question'
Tennessee Williams

How Can We Have Faith?

Introduction

'... those who become Christians become new persons. They are not the same anymore, for the old is gone. A new life has begun!' New Living Bible, 2 Corinthians 5:17

But we all have different experiences, so how can we be sure of our faith?

God is three persons in one – the Father, the Son and the Holy Spirit – we call this the Trinity.

Each member of the Trinity – Father, Son and Holy Spirit – has a part to play in helping us to be sure of our faith.

03

WHAT THE FATHER PROMISES

It is safer to rely on God's promises in the Bible than on our changeable feelings.
God's promises to us:

'I will come in'
(Revelation 3:20) – he is waiting to start a relationship with us

'I am always with you'
(Matthew 28:20) – he never leaves us even for a moment

'I give them eternal life'
(John 10:28) – we have the great hope of heaven to look forward to

FAITH = taking God's promises and daring to believe them.

WHAT JESUS DID

John 3:16

We can never earn God's forgiveness but Jesus died to destroy the barrier between God and us.

God loves us and died to prove it

He took our sins upon himself

'You think about people, but God thinks about you'
Tolstoy

'I want to know God's thoughts, the rest are details'

Albert Einstein

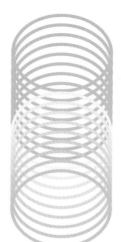

WHAT THE SPIRIT DOES

Romans 8:9

When someone becomes a Christian God's Holy Spirit comes to live within them.

The Holy Spirit inside of us changes us from the inside out:

Our character / personality

Our relationship with God and with other people

'The Holy Spirit inside of me also helps me to be sure that I am God's child.'

Complete Inadequacy meets Total Adequacy

Inadequacy, it's part of the human condition – perhaps, particularly of the teenage condition. It certainly feels like it. A time in life when challenges bear down on you like freight trains, and it seems that every time a challenge arrives the stakes are higher than the time before. There are exams that must be passed, interviews in which you must impress, members of the opposite sex whom you must attract, life-style choices that must be made, and purchases that must be bought with money that had to be earned. No wonder we are sometimes reduced to gibbering wrecks, and sometimes lock ourselves in our darkened bedrooms and listen to depressing music.

In the midst of all that the last thing you need is religion, right? I mean that's just another set of rules that must be kept, another 1001 ways to fail and mess up. Isn't it?

Fortunately not, not with Christianity at least.

While 'success' in other religions might revolve around the efforts of the worshipper, Christianity is all about God. It's not about how much we pray, not about our fasting or going on pilgrimages, not about our keeping the rules and impressing God. It's about God, the Father, moved by love, reaching out to us in all of our weakness and inadequacy. It's about God, in Jesus, acting to put things right between us. And about God's Holy Spirit filling us and assuring us of his love and helping us change into the kind of people we've always wanted to be.

Being sure of our faith is realising that our complete inadequacy is swallowed up in God's total adequacy ✻

Primary Sources

'This resurrection life you received from God is not a timid, grave-tending life. It's adventurously expectant, greeting God with a childlike "What's next, Papa?" God's Spirit touches our spirits and confirms who we really are: Father and children. And we know we are going to get what is coming to us – an unbelievable inheritance! We go through exactly what Christ goes through. If we go through the hard times with him, then we're certainly going to go through the good times with him!'

'Can a mother forget the baby at her breast and have no compassion on the child she has borne? Though she may forget, I will not forget you!'

God

TRINITY

Back before The Matrix (where 'Trinity' is a beautiful woman dressed all in black who falls in love with Neo) 'Trinity' referred to God.

While the word itself never appears in the Bible it is clear from the New Testament that the only way to understand who God is is to recognise that he is three persons in one substance. If you don't feel quite able to wrap you mind around that don't worry, you're not alone. For two thousand years the greatest brains of the church have been trying to establish exactly what 'Trinity' means and trying to describe it to the common people like you and me.

Whilst things might be fuzzy around the margins one thing we can definitely learn from the 'doctrine of the Trinity', as it is known, is the central importance to all of life, to all of us, of relationship. From an understanding of God as Trinity we can see that through all eternity, in the aeons before the world was made, the three persons of God lived in love – in perfect relationship, perfect community, or, to use a more religious sounding word, in 'perfect communion'.

The whole purpose and action of God in history, in creation, in covenant, in redemption was to draw others – and that includes us – into this perfect relationship ✳

Conclusion

We can be sure that our faith is true.

1 John 5:13

This is not arrogant or proud because we are not trusting in ourselves. We are trusting in God: his promises to us; his work to free us from sin; and his Holy Spirit changing us from the inside out.

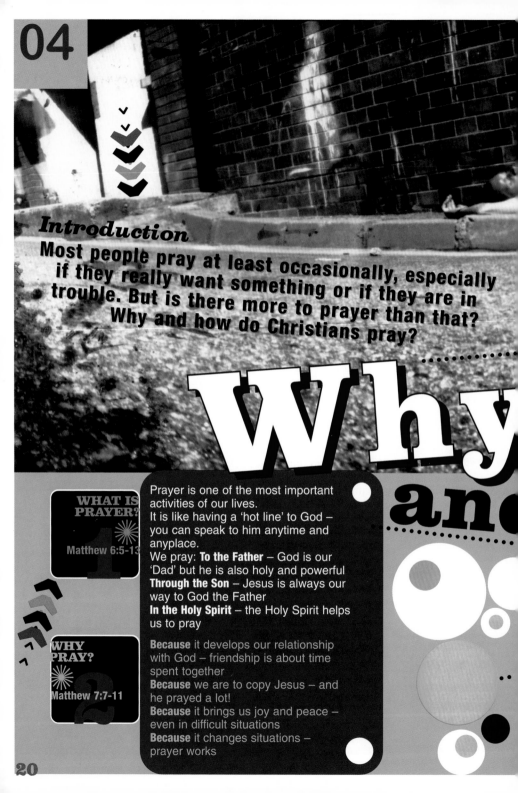

Introduction

Most people pray at least occasionally, especially if they really want something or if they are in trouble. But is there more to prayer than that? Why and how do Christians pray?

Why and

WHAT IS PRAYER?
1
Matthew 6:5-13

Prayer is one of the most important activities of our lives.
It is like having a 'hot line' to God – you can speak to him anytime and anyplace.
We pray: **To the Father** – God is our 'Dad' but he is also holy and powerful
Through the Son – Jesus is always our way to God the Father
In the Holy Spirit – the Holy Spirit helps us to pray

WHY PRAY?
2
Matthew 7:7-11

Because it develops our relationship with God – friendship is about time spent together
Because we are to copy Jesus – and he prayed a lot!
Because it brings us joy and peace – even in difficult situations
Because it changes situations – prayer works

'Prayer is ...' (Christian teenagers define prayer)

'Prayer is communicating with God'

'Prayer is time for us to get to know God and to talk to him'

'Prayer is like a telephone for us to talk to Jesus'

'Prayer is like chatting to a best-friend who just happens to be in control of everything'

'Prayer is being yourself with God'

'Prayer is hearing, sensing, listening, experiencing – between person and God'

'Prayer is more than just talking to God – being with him as he is and as you are'

'Prayer is like taking time out with God'

'Prayer is going from feeling awful as you go through all the ridiculously stupid things you've done that day, to feeling fantastic as you think about how it's all completely wiped clean by God.'

HOW DO I Pray?

DOES GOD ALWAYS ANSWER MY PRAYERS?

1 John 3:21-22

We can let things create a barrier between us and God:

* if we are disobedient * if we don't forgive
* if we haven't told God about the things
we've done wrong * if our motives are wrong

Sometimes we want things that are not good for us – God will only give us what is best for us.

Remember that 'Yes' 'No' and 'Wait' are all answers.

HOW DO WE PRAY?

1 Thessalonians 5:17

To help us to pray we can follow a pattern:

T * THANK YOU * praise God for all he has given you
S * SORRY * admit to God what you have done wrong
P * PLEASE * ask God for what you and others need

You can pray anytime and any place, while doing anything. **But ...** it is good to have a regular time when you can pray alone and not be distracted, and times when you can learn to pray with other people.

REAL LIFE STORIES

ANNA
aged 17

'I can tell you that God is alive because I talked to him this morning'

Billy Graham

Primary Sources

'THE LORD'S PRAYER IN THREE INCARNATIONS'

Traditional

'Our Father which art in heaven,
Hallowed be Thy name.
Thy kingdom come.
Thy will be done in earth as it is in heaven.
Give us this day our daily bread.
And forgive us our debts as we forgive our debtors.
And lead us not into temptation, but deliver us from evil:
For Thine is the kingdom, and the power, and the glory forever.
Amen.

(Matthew 6:9-13 King James Version)

Contemporary

'Our Father in heaven,
Reveal who you are,.
Set the world right;
Do what's best –
as above, so below.
Keep us alive with three square meals.
Keep us forgiven with you and forgiving others.
Keep us safe from ourselves and the Devil.
You're in charge!
You can do anything you want!
You're ablaze in beauty!
Yes. Yes. Yes.

(Matthew 6:9-13 THE MESSAGE)

Text message version

dad@hvn
urspshl.
wewant wot u want
@urth2b like hvn.
giv us food
&4giv r sins lyk we
4giv uvaz.
don't test us!save us!
bcos we kno ur boss,
ur tuf&ur cool
4eva!
ok?

Someone prayed to God for me that I would know when I did something that God didn't like, because I felt that I was doing bad things and didn't even think they were wrong. And then the next day I went to the pub during school, basically, and it didn't even occur to me that it was wrong. Seriously, I don't understand how I could be that naive. But I was there and I was talking to friends and they started saying, 'You could get expelled for this.' I was thinking, oh, maybe I shouldn't have done it. And then God crossed my mind, and I thought, 'Oh, does God mind me doing this?' As soon as I felt that I tried to push it out, but I had this really heavy feeling with me for an hour. Then, going home on the bus, I was talking to God. I was saying, 'OK, what's wrong?' Then, as soon as I said, 'OK, fine. I won't do that kind of thing again.' I just felt completely free and that whole heavy feeling had gone. I knew that God had answered the prayer. He had shown me that what I was doing was wrong and had shown me what I had to do different ✳'

Introduction

The Bible is a big book: in fact 66 books and over 750,000 words all inside one cover. ✳The Bible is the most popular book in the world. ✳ The Bible is the most powerful book in the world. ✳ The Bible is the most precious book in the world. **But not many of us really know much about it, or about how to get the best out of it.**

Why and Ho
I Read the

'There are an average of 6.8 Bibles in every American household'

AN INSTRUCTION MANUAL FOR LIFE
✳
2 Timothy 3:15-17

Key fact this is no ordinary book. The Bible is uniquely God's book. The Bible is 'God-breathed' or 'God-inspired'. Even though humans wrote the words, it was God who inspired and guided them.

The Bible can teach us

The Bible can correct us when we are living wrongly

The Bible can show us how to live for God

w Should
Bible?

'Forget the modern British novelists and TV tie-ins; the Bible is the biggest-selling book every year' **The Times**

'It is estimated that 44 million Bibles are sold every year'

> > >>>

A WAY TO RELATION-SHIP

John 5:39-40

God speaks to us through the Bible:
God speaks before we are Christians to bring us to salvation through faith in Jesus

God speaks to us when we are Christians

✳ helps us to become more like Jesus

✳ helps us when the going gets tough

✳ helps us to know what is the right way

✳ helps us towards health and healing

✳ helps us beat evil

✳ helps us to be clean on the inside

✳ helps us by giving power

HOW DO WE HEAR GOD SPEAK THROUGH THE BIBLE?

Choose a time when you are not rushed or stressed – if possible make this a regular habit.

Choose a place where you are relaxed and where you won't be disturbed.

Begin by praying: ask God to speak to you through what you read.

Don't just switch off and let your mind wander.

Ask yourself:

What does this say?
What does this mean?
How should this affect me?

Put what you have read and learned into practice.

Read it, learn from it, but most of all, enjoy it.

Primary Sources

'There's nothing like the written Word of God for showing you the way to salvation through faith in Christ Jesus. Every part of Scripture is God-breathed and useful one way or another – showing us truth, exposing our rebellion, correcting our mistakes, training us to live God's way. Through the Word we are put together and shaped for the tasks God has for us.'

Timothy 3:16-17 THE MESSAGE

Unpicking the code?

Now the Bible is a great book, no doubt about it. But if anyone tells you that it's an easy book to apply to life in the 21 Century, or that hearing God speak through it is without complication then you are in the presence of what used to be called a charlatan – today we might say that they deal in bull...excrement. Just listen to these older teenagers discussing their experience of the Bible ...

Annabel (aged 16) is, perhaps the most honest. 'I think every time I've tried reading the Bible it's sort of ... baffling for me. I dunno, it's quite hard to understand so I end up not reading it for a while. I haven't actually read the Bible for quite a long time.'

Even those who really believe in the power of the Bible recognise that there is work that must be done before it can be applied to life.

'People say it's [the Bible] irrelevant but I think that's such rubbish 'cos it's really very, very relevant – as long as you can un-pick the code as it were ...' (Tom, aged 17).

Part of un-picking the code is about being smart enough to know when you're beaten and when you are in need of help.

Anna (aged 17): 'I find that often I get confused, I'll read something and I'll go, "Wot?" and it will get me really puzzling over why I believe this kind of thing. And usually I've got it completely wrong. I'll go and talk to someone who really knows about it and when I talk to them it completely makes sense. I think the Bible is obviously really cool but you've got to get help.'

Izzat (aged 18) and Paula (aged 16) have found that using Bible reading notes written especially to help young people apply the Bible has really helped.

At the end of the day, when we've done all we can God, by his Holy Spirit in us, can help us to see the relevance of his book to our lives.

REAL LIFE STORIES

'The Bible is high explosive'

British Prime Minister Stanley Baldwin

The last word goes to Gemma (aged 17): 'It's relevant to our lives with loads of issues from relationships to money to family. But I think with the Bible you've really got to pray, combine it with prayer. You've got to ask God to help you apply it to your life☀'

It was Valentine's night. I had been to a party and was sitting in my room at college when my greatest friend came back with his girlfriend (now his wife) and told me that they had become Christians. I was immediately alarmed about them, thinking that the Moonies had got them and they needed my help.

I was at times an atheist, and at times an agnostic, unsure of what I believed. I had been baptised and confirmed, but it had not meant much to me. At school I had been to chapel regularly and studied the Bible in RE lessons. But I had ended up rejecting it all and, indeed, arguing powerfully (or so I thought) against Christianity.

Now I wanted to help my friends, so I thought I would embark on a thorough research of the subject. I made a plan to read the Koran, Karl Marx,

Jean-Paul Sartre (the existentialist philosopher) and the Bible. I happened to have a rather dusty copy of the Bible on my shelves, so that night I picked it up and started reading. I read all the way through Matthew, Mark and Luke, and halfway through John's Gospel. Then I fell asleep. When I

woke up, I finished John's Gospel and carried on through Acts, Romans and 1 and 2 Corinthians. I was completely gripped by what I read. I had read it before and it had meant virtually nothing to me. This time it came alive and I could not put it down. It had a ring of truth about it. I knew as I read it that I had to respond because it spoke so powerfully to me. Very shortly afterwards I came to put my faith in Jesus Christ☀

'The Bible's beautifully personal and its been really helpful to me just to listen and to learn to hear God through it' **Phil, aged 22**

06

'God guides me mostly by the things that I feel most deeply and passionately about in my stomach. When I feel I really want to do something more deeply than anything else, I say, 'OK, do you want me to do this God?' And he seems to answer me.' *Hannah*

How Does

INTRODUCTION * Jeremiah 29:11

We all have to make decisions: if we are sensible we seek guidance.
God promises to guide us when we ask him.
God has a good plan for each of us.
It is wise to involve God in all of our big decisions.
Without God we are likely to get into a mess.
God guides us in many different ways: > >> 〉〉〉

The Bible is full of general guidelines about how we should live our lives – we should always follow these.
God also speaks to us through the Bible about specific situations.
If we make a habit of studying the Bible regularly then God will often bring a particular verse to light at just the right time to help guide us in a decision.

THROUGH THE BIBLE
Timothy 3:16
1

God Guide us?

THROUGH THE HOLY SPIRIT

Acts 13:1-3

The Holy Spirit helps us to recognise God's voice.
God speaks as we pray – he might give us a strong sense of what is right. ✳he might give us a strong desire to do something ✳he might bring a thought to our minds.

We must test our feelings:
Is it loving towards others? Will it bring God's peace?
Sometimes the Holy Spirit speaks in more unusual ways: prophecy; visions and pictures; dreams; angels; a voice that can be heard.

THROUGH COMMON SENSE

Psalm 32:8-9

God wants us to use our brains to think about the consequences of our choices.

29

Primary Sources

The congregation in Antioch was blessed with a number of prophet-preachers and teachers: Barnabus, Simon, nicknamed Niger, Lucius the Cyrenian, Manaen, an advisor to the ruler Herod, Saul.

One day as they were worshipping God – they were also fasting as they waited for guidance – the Holy Spirit spoke: "Take Barnabus and Saul and commission them for the work I have called them to do." So they commissioned them. In that circle of intensity and obedience, of fasting and praying, they laid hands on their heads and sent them off.'

(Acts 13:1-3 THE MESSAGE)

THROUGH ADVICE FROM OTHERS

Proverbs 12:15-17

The wiser you are the more aware you will be that you need help to make the most of life.

THROUGH CIRCUM-STANCES

Proverbs 16:9

Our eyes should be open to opportunities and to closed doors. But sometimes we need to keep going in spite of difficulty.

REAL LIFE
PHIL STORIES

A time that God guided me ... It wasn't an active process really, it was more that God guided me into something. It was my year-off between school and university.

I hadn't sorted out anything to do; I had just left it completely – being really unorganised.

I had been given an application form by my tutor at school two years before, when I was sixteen. I'd just kept it in a drawer because it was for short-term mission work and I didn't want to do that. The form was really scary. It asked things like, 'Which church do you go to?' and I didn't go to one.

Anyway, I ran out of options, filled that form out – really patchily, I barely put anything on it – and got the last place to go away to the

MUSCULAR GUIDANCE

'Their plan was to turn west into Asia province, but the Holy Spirit blocked that route. So they went to Mysia and tried to go north to Bithnyia, but the Spirit of Jesus wouldn't let them go there either.' **(Acts 16:6-7)**

I can't read that passage without thinking Gridiron (that's American Football to the uninitiated). It's as though Paul and his companions are trying to execute a great little running play across Asia. But as soon as they take the hand-off and prepare to sprint downfield there's a hulking great defensive lineman, with 'Holy Spirit' emblazoned across his shirt, blocking the way.

Change of plan ... Roll out of the tackle and break right, hoping to head down the touchline towards Bithnyia. Then comes the biggest, fastest, most skilled linebacker the game has ever seen. The Spirit of Jesus closes in. There's no opening in that direction either.

It's what you might call a 'muscular' form of guidance that God is using to get Paul and his mission team where he wants them. It's only later when their initial plans lie in ruins that Paul has the dream that tells him where they should be going.

In a way, the story is encouraging. Paul and his team were getting on with what they believed God wanted of them. They had good news to share, and they were using their brains to put a plan in place, and they were prepared to sweat as much as necessary to put the plan into action. Their habit was to get on with it and trust that God would put them right if they drifted off course or if he had other, better ideas. That's exactly what happened. What that means to us, I think, is that we can relax a bit. Our job is to do what God has placed before us – be that school, work, relationships or service – as best we can; using our brains and our energy to the full.

If God has other plans or ideas then we can be confident that he will step-in in as muscular a manner as is necessary to put us back on course ✳

Conclusion ✳ Don't rush decisions – sometimes we have to wait. Remember that we all make mistakes – but God forgives.

selection weekend, and the last place to go on the trip.

I ended up going for four months to Ecuador and when I got there I just knew that it was so right that I was there.

It was amazing because it happened not by my own thinking or sorting but by God leading me there ✳'

Who Is the Holy Spirit?

Introduction * The Holy Spirit has remained masked and misunderstood for too long. He is the third person of the Trinity – Father, Son and Holy Spirit. * It is easier for us to picture the Father, or Jesus the Son, so we want to ask, 'Who is the Holy Spirit?' * To do this we are going to take a quick tour through the Bible, starting at the very beginning...

> > >>>>

HE WAS INVOLVED IN CREATION

Genesis 1:2

The Holy Spirit is known as the breath of God

✱ He was involved in the creation of the universe

✱ He breathed life into humans.

PARTICULAR PEOPLE, PARTICULAR TIMES, PARTICULAR TASKS

Isaiah 61:3

> > >>>>

> > >>>>

THE HOLY SPIRIT WAS PROMISED BY THE FATHER

Ezekiel 36:26-27

In the Old Testament the Holy Spirit gave people power:

✱ to express themselves in art
✱ to lead
✱ to perform feats of great strength
✱ to prophesy

God promised that at the right time the Holy Spirit would come in a new way. The Holy Spirit would not just be on some people, some of the time, but on the inside of all believers all of the time.

JESUS AND THE HOLY SPIRIT

Luke 3:15-22

Around the time of Jesus the Holy Spirit became very busy.
John the Baptist announced that someone was coming who would baptise people with the Holy Spirit.
At Jesus' baptism the Holy Spirit came down on him and he received power.
Jesus predicted that his disciples would receive the Holy Spirit, but still they had to wait ...

Primary Sources

'But John intervened: "I'm baptising you here in the river. The main character in this drama, to whom I'm a mere stagehand, will ignite the kingdom life, a fire, the Holy Spirit within you, changing you from the inside out. He's going to clean house – make a clean sweep of your lives. He'll place everything true in its proper place before God; everything false he'll put out with the trash to be burned."
...
After all the people were baptised, Jesus was baptised. As he was praying, the sky opened up and the Holy Spirit, like a dove descending, came down on him. And along with the Spirit, a voice: "You are my Son, chosen and marked by my love, pride of my life.'

(Luke 3:16-17; 21-22 THE MESSAGE)

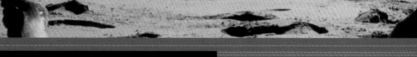

CONCLUSION* Acts 2:38-3!

After Jesus' death, resurrection and ascension into heaven the H
On the day of Pentecost
The disciples spoke in new languages, received a new boldness a
Today the Holy Spirit is available to all of

REAL LIFE STORIES

Who are you and what do you do?
My name is Hannah and I work from home as a graphic designer.

Have you always been into arty and creative things?
Suppose I've always been quite creative, whether I've been drawing, travelling or just doing day-to-day life stuff.

Do you feel the Holy Spirit has a role in your creativity?
Yeah, we're all made in very diverse ways. Each person is instinctively enthusiastic about something different. I think that it was when God was designing and inventing people that we acquired the desire to create things also. Hmmm, the Holy Spirit must have designed the human race then. We sort of imitate him 'cos we're made like he is, we can't help it. The Holy Spirit lives inside me. I ask the Holy Spirit to inspire me because he has designed amazing things... I mean, just look at a mountain, or a person's eye, or the sky on a clear night... his designs are loads better than ours. But when we know him we have access to his ideas simply because he wants to share himself with us, he wants the best for us and then others are inspired too.

How does this influence the way you go about your work?
Well, I know that I've got someone close to me who knows the secrets of the best designs in the world. I ask him to let me know how to design like him. I ask the Holy Spirit to do his will through my work. The Holy Spirit is beautiful and if we open our innermost parts to him he can reveal his beauty through our lives whether we design, paint, sing, dance or write. Opening up to him is a little bit like when you begin to trust someone with your secrets – little by little. It's a very gentle thing to experience. He never forces you. It's about letting yourself be loved. It's sometimes painful because you are being honest, but it's worth it ※
   (Editors Note: Hannah is the designer of this manual.)

irit finally arrived.
sciples were filled with the Holy Spirit in a completely new way.
v power.
can breathe new life into us and give us power to live for God.

"I know a church where we could go and talk"

Do you need help carrying your bible? It looks heavy.

NOVEMBER 26. 1948

What are your plans for tonight? Feel like a bible study?

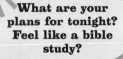

"God told me to come and talk to you"

HERE are illustrations of the full series of our styles in the Stock Block service. ...rs will find these stock blocks invaluable ...rating their local press advertisements, ..., letterheads, etc. There are at pre-

STOCK
sent thirteen different ...
we illustrate individually

Christians don't shake hands, Christians hug.

"Do you want to come over and watch the 10 commandments tonight?"

Did it hurt when you fell from Heaven?

Is it a sin that you stole my heart?

The Bible says "Give drink to those who are thirsty, and feed the hungry", how about dinner?

are available 3in. deep by approximately 1in. wide (as illustrated), and priced at 19s Readers requiring stock blocks sh to " Stock Blocks," Tailor and C Gerrard Street, London, W. 1

14

'I know men and I tel
mere man. Between hii
in the world there
comparison. Alexande:
and I founded our empi:
rest the creation of our :
Christ founded his emp
hour millions of men w

you **Jesus Christ** is no
and every other person
no possible term of
Caesar, Charlemagne
s, but upon what did we
nius? Upon force. **Jesus**
e upon love and at this
ld die for him.'

Napoleon Bonaparte

weekend
weekend
weekend
weekend
ekend

'Prince Charles has many titles. He is the Heir Apparent to the Crown, his Royal Highness, the Prince of Wales, Duke of Cornwall, Knight of the Garter, Colonel in Chief of the Royal Regiment of Wales, Duke of Rothesay, Knight of the Thistle, Great Master of the Order of Bath, Earl of Chester, Earl of Carrick, Baron of Renfrew, Lord of the Isles and Great Steward of Scotland. We would address him as "Your Royal Highness", but I suspect that to William and Harry he is just "Dad".When we become children of God we have an intimacy with our heavenly King.'

Nicky Gumbel

What Does the
Holy Spirit
Do
?

Introduction John 3:5-7*
Just as we are physically born into a human family – so
the Holy Spirit gives us a new birth into God's family.

SONS AND DAUGHTERS OF GOD
1
Romans 8:14-17

GETTING TO KNOW GOD BETTER
2
Ephesians 1:17-18

GROWING IN THE FAMILY LIKENESS
3
2 Corinthians 3:17-18

We are forgiven
for all that we
have done
wrong.
We become
God's children.

The Holy Spirit
helps us to pray.
The Holy Spirit
helps us to
understand the
Bible.

The Holy Spirit
helps us to
become more
like Jesus
– in every part of
our lives.
– in every way.

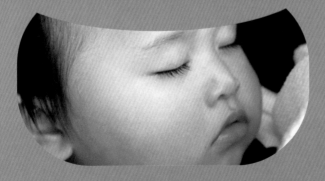

Primary Sources

'Whenever, though, they turn to face God as Moses did, God removes the ve
and there they are - face to face! They suddenly recognise that God is a
living, personal presence, not a piece of chiseled stone. And when God i
personally present, a living Spirit, that old, constricting legislation is
recognised as obsolete. We're free of it! All of us! Nothing between u
and God, our faces shining with the brightness of his face. And so we ar
transfigured much like the Messiah, our lives gradually becoming brighter
and more beautiful as God enters our lives and we become like him.'

(2 Corinthians 3:16-18 THE MESSAGE)

ONE BIG FAMILY
Ephesians 4:3-6

GIFTS FOR ALL THE CHILDREN
1 Corinthians 12

A GROWING FAMILY
Acts 1:8

The same Holy Spirit lives within every Christian regardless of nationality, church, age, location.
We are all one family.

Just like a human parent, God loves to give gifts to his children.
God also knows that each of his children is different and so he gives different gifts to each child.
The gifts that God gives are for us to use to help the rest of the family.

The Holy Spirit gives us the power to live for Jesus.
The Holy Spirit gives us the courage to tell others so that they can join the family.

CONCLUSION* Ephesians 5:18-20

Every Christian has the Holy Spirit living in them.
Not every Christian is filled with the Holy Spirit.
The Bible says, 'Be filled with the Spirit'

REAL LIFE STORIES

Jane is a 19-year-old second year student at Warwick University studying for a degree in Education.

'My parents aren't Christians but my uncle and aunt became Christians about 10 years ago and I had always been quite curious about it but not enough to start going to church. I used to help out at the local Sunday School but more because I wanted to look after little children than to find out more about God.

At Warwick University I made friends with a girl called Emma who is a Christian and when she heard the students were running an Alpha course she wanted someone to go along with her and so I said I'd give it a try.

There were 100 people there and you could tell there were a lot of Christians because they were so kind. They came up and talked to me and weren't too pushy. It was a brilliant atmosphere.

We got some food and then sat down and listened to the first talk. It was very thought provoking and then we had the discussion groups which I thought were great.

They were composed of about 50-50 Christians and non-Christians.

I thought I'd carry on for the first couple of weeks and if nothing came of it then at least it would have been useful for me in relation to teaching RE. But I continued to be really impressed by the Christians I'd met and how their lives had been changed. They were so calm and I really felt I wanted to be a part of what they had. But I wanted a positive sign. I prayed and prayed but nothing seemed to happen.

Then on the Holy Spirit day we were talking in our discussion group and I suddenly started to cry. I kept on crying and the group prayed for me. And then I stopped crying and I knew I believed from that moment. I felt intensely warm.

I had wanted to believe for so long and suddenly I did ✳

talk3

How Can I
With the H

As strong Christians we need to be filled with the Holy Spirit

WHAT HAPPENS WHEN PEOPLE EXPERIENCE THE HOLY SPIRIT?
Acts 10:23-48

The Book of Acts is the story of the start of the Christian church

At Pentecost the disciples were filled with the Holy Spirit for the first time and they felt his power.

In Samaria the Holy Spirit's work was so dramatic that the local magician tried to buy his power!

When Paul received the Holy Spirit he got his sight back.

In Ephesus the people were able to speak God's messages in a new way through the Spirit.

In the house of Cornelius the Roman:

✳ everyone knew when the people received the Holy Spirit.

✳ everyone was freed to praise God.

✳ everyone was given a new language of praise.

This new language is sometimes called the gift of tongues.

It is a special language for prayer.

We can use it to pray for ourselves, for others, and to worship God.

Be Filled with the Holy Spirit?

CAN ANYTHING STOP US BEING FILLED?
Luke 11:9-13

God wants to fill all his children with his Holy Spirit, but sometimes we put up barriers that make it difficult for us to be filled.

We doubt that God wants to give us such a good gift – but he does!

We get scared – but God loves us and his gifts are good!

We doubt we're worthy of the gift – but God promises to give to any who ask him!

When the Feast of Pentecost came, they were all together in one place. Without warning there was a sound like a strong wind, gale force – no one could tell where it came from. It filled the whole building. Then, like a wildfire, the Holy Spirit spread through their ranks, and they started speaking in a number of different languages as the Spirit prompted them.'

(Acts 2:1-4 THE MESSAGE)

MARK
aged 17

REAL LIFE STORIES

'We moved to New Bern, North Carolina about two years ago. I had some friends who went to Faith Methodist Church, so we started going there.

I did your normal teenage things. We went to parties and did things we shouldn't do. I tried a little bit of illegal drugs. I didn't think it was that great a problem.

The biggest problem was when a friend I was with got in trouble with law enforcement.

I realised we weren't doing the right things. My friend's dad talked to me about Alpha. His son had to do it [as part of a judicial sentence] and he asked me if I would participate too.

I loved it. I looked forward to doing it. It gave me a whole new perspective on being a Christian and information on how to back up my beliefs.

I had always seen what people said was the Holy Spirit, but I never experienced it. On the Saturday of the Holy Spirit retreat weekend, we watched a video about receiving the Holy Spirit.

After it was over our pastor asked if there was anyone who would like to receive the Holy Spirit. Some people went up and he prayed over them and you could feel something start to enter the room, this amazing peaceful presence.

I found myself drawn forward, almost compelled to go forward. It started like a tingle and then I felt waves of power starting to flow through me. It felt like a great peace. As I truly repented, he cleansed me and made me new.

For most of my life I have been sitting on the fence between salvation and damnation, without knowing the danger this imposes. My life from there on has been so amazing. I have the guidelines and foundation on which to live.

Alpha gave me tools. I always felt I was a Christian, but I realised I hadn't been doing the things God wants me to do.

I am on fire for God. The gradual movement towards what God wants for me has become a full sprint' ✳

fr⊖⊖dom

At a time of life when you are
striving for independence it might seem
odd to be thinking about handing over control of
your life to God; especially to the extent of inviting the
Holy Spirit to come and fill you and change you from the
inside out. Doesn't that deny all the freedoms – to make your own
choices, to live your own life, to set your own goals – that you've
battled your parents or guardians for over the past years?
The answer is No. Giving our lives over to God increases our freedom.
Let me illustrate with a strange little story about an independently-minded, in
fact downright rebellious guitar string. (If you need to impress in English class,
imagining an inanimate object like a guitar string acting in a human-like way is called
anthropomorphism.)
Anyway, the rebellious / independent guitar string had had enough of being laid out
straight next to five others like him, had had enough of being stretched tighter and
tighter and then mercilessly strummed and plucked by the musician.
'I'm going to escape,' he declared, and proceeded to twist and turn, compress and
stretch, push and pull until he was free of all constraint and fell with a 'twang' to the floor.
For a while the string was in string heaven. The freedom he had! He could twist and
turn, and bounce and bound to his heart's content. There was no one to draw him
uncomfortably tight, no one to pinch, pluck, press or strum him. He was free.
Except, as time wore on he came to realise that he was free to do anything he
wanted, except the thing that he had been made for. He could no longer make
music.

There are, perhaps, two types of freedom – one negative and one positive.
The negative kind is simply the absence of restrictions, rules and
constraints. The positive kind is the freedom to achieve all that you
can, the freedom to make the most of your life, or as the US Armed
Forces put it to 'be all that you can be'.
Allowing ourselves to be filled by the Holy Spirit and
submitting ourselves to God and his ways is the
way to make the most of our lives and be
all that we can be ✳

CONCLUSION

**It's not enough to talk about being filled with God's Holy Spirit.
We also need to give God the chance to fill us.**

How Can I Resist

> > >>>> **INTRODUCTION**
Christians believe that just as God is
the source of all that is good and
beautiful so the devil is behind all evil
and horror.

WHY SHOULD WE BELIEVE IN THE DEVIL?
Luke 10:17-20

✳Because the Bible speaks of him – in the Old Testament and the New Testament.
✳Because Christians have believed in him down the ages.
✳Because it is clear from the horror and evil in our world that he is at work.
✳BUT – it is just as dangerous to take too much of an interest in the devil as to doubt that he even exists.

WHAT DOES THE DEVIL HAVE TO DO WITH ME?
John 10:10

✳The devil aims to destroy all humans.
✳He tries to blind our eyes so that we cannot see God.
✳He tries to feed doubts into our minds.
✳He tries to tempt us to do wrong.

SHOULD I BE WORRIED?
Colossians 1:13
3

✳No! Jesus has won a complete victory over the devil.
✳We can live in Jesus' kingdom and not the devil's kingdom.
✳In Jesus' kingdom there is:
> forgiveness instead of sin.
> freedom instead of slavery.
> life instead of death.
> salvation instead of destruction.

HOW DO WE DEFEND OURSELVES?
Ephesians 6:11-17
4

The book of Ephesians in the New Testament describes the armour that God has given us:
The belt of truth – knowing Jesus' truth to counter the devil's lies
The breastplate of righteousness – believing Jesus can protect us from guilt
The boots of the gospel of peace – being ready to speak about Jesus
The shield of faith – being sure of God's promises
The helmet of salvation – protecting our minds from doubts
The sword of the Spirit – getting to know the Bible and attacking the devil with its truth

HOW DO WE ATTACK?
2 Corinthians 10:4
5

By praying – the devil trembles when we pray.
By action – we attack the devil by doing the things that Jesus told us to do.

REAL LIFE STORIES

'EVIL IS ...'

(Christian teenagers define evil)

'Evil is hating people when you should be loving them instead'

'Evil is something that gets in between you and doing what is right'

'Evil is something we come across everyday'

'Evil is the devil, always trying to stop us coming closer to God'

'Evil is September 11th'

'Evil is un-love'

'Evil is really subtle and insidious and always seems to get you when you least expect it'

'Evil is things which tempt me when I know they are wrong'

'Evil is very, very bad. Stay away from it!'

'Evil is to do with small things, like spiteful stuff in relationships, but then it can flower into wars and stuff like that'

When I was really young I d something that really, really wish I hadn done. I went to a fortune teller with a friend. We were young, only in Primary School. The fortune teller told me something that to this day is always in my head. I hate it.' Gemma's experience is a good example of why the Bible warns Christians to steer clear of all kinds of 'occult' practices, including the ones – li fortune telling, horoscopes, white witchcraft and ouija – that can seem harmless.

What the Bible explains is that any kind of spiritual power that does not come directly from God through Jesus is dangerous and ultimately evil.

If you have been involved in these things talk to a Christian that you respect and trust and have them pray with you.

Primary Sources

'Later the Master selected seventy and sent them ahead of him in pairs to every town and place where he intended to go... The seventy came back triumphant. "Master, even the demons danced to your tune!" Jesus said, "I know. I saw Satan fall, a bolt of lightning out of the sky. See what I've given you? Safe passage as you walk on snakes and scorpions, and protection from every assault of the Enemy. No one can put a hand on you. All the same, the great triumph is not in your authority over evil, but in God's authority over you and presence with you. Not what you do for God but what God does for you – that's the agenda for rejoicing.'

(Luke 10:1; 17-20 THE MESSAGE)

Nature of potential danger

Ask God to forgive you for involving yourself with these spiritual powers, and ask him to set you free from them. Make a point of getting rid of any articles (books, videos, etc.) that you have that are connected with this kind of practice.

It is important to stress the greatness of God and the relative powerlessness of the enemy.

In C. S. Lewis's book The Great Divorce a man has arrived in heaven and is being shown around by his 'teacher'. He goes down on his hands and knees, takes a blade of grass and, using the thin end as a pointer, he eventually finds a tiny crack in the soil in which is concealed the whole of hell:

'Do you mean then that Hell – all that infinite empty town – is down some little crack like this?

'Yes. All Hell is smaller than one pebble of your earthly world: but it is smaller than one atom of this world, the Real World. Look at yon butterfly. If it swallowed all Hell, Hell would not be big enough to do any harm or to have any taste.'

'It seems big enough when you are in it, Sir.'

'And

yet all loneliness, angers, hatreds, envies and itchings that it contains, if rolled into one single experience and put into the scale against the least moment of the joy that is felt by the least in Heaven, would have no weight that could be registered at all. Bad cannot succeed even in being bad as truly as good is good. If all Hell's miseries together entered the consciousness of yon wee yellow bird on the bough there, they would be swallowed up without trace, as if one drop of ink had been dropped into that Great Ocean to which your terrestrial Pacific itself is only a molecule' ☀

(As quoted in Questions of Life pages 169-70)

Conclusion* Colossians 2:15

The devil is real and so is his influence in the world, but he is no match for God. We have no cause to fear the devil because we are now in Jesus' kingdom. There is no reason for great interest in the devil. Why worry about a loser?

Why and How Should I Tell Others?

INTRODUCTION
*Matthew 28:16-20

We should tell others:
because Jesus told us to.
because everyone has a built-in need for Jesus.
because it is good news.

Danger: of being insensitive to others or of being fearful of others.
Key: to trust God and to have a good relationship with the person you wish to tell.

LIVE THE MESSAGE
Matthew 5:13-16

1

When people know that we are Christians they watch how we live – our actions should match our words.

TALK THE MESSAGE
2 Corinthians 5-11

2

When we talk about what we believe, people will ask questions.

We should be ready to answer – reading Christian books and especially the Bible will help.

PRESENT THE MESSAGE
John 1:39-42

3

Not everyone will be a great preacher – but everyone can be a 'witness' to Jesus.

POWER THE MESSAGE
Acts 3

4

In the New Testament God used miracles to back up the message.

God still does miracles today and we shouldn't be afraid to ask him to show his power to people.

PRAY THE MESSAGE
Acts 4:29-31

5

Prayer is essential – ✴pray that people's eyes would be opened to see the truth about God. ✴pray that God would give us boldness to talk about our faith.

Primary Sources

'Let me tell you why you are here. You are here to be salt-seasoning that brings out the God-flavours of this earth. If you lose your saltiness, how will people taste godliness? You've lost your usefulness and will end up in the garbage.

Here's another way to put it: You're here to be light, bringing out the God-colours in the world. God is not a secret to be kept. We're going public with this, as public as a city on a hill. If I make you light-bearers, you don't think I'm going to hide you under a bucket, do you? I'm putting you on a light stand. Now that I've put you there on a hilltop, on a light stand - shine! Keep open house; be generous with your lives. By opening up to others you'll prompt people to open up with God, this generous Father in heaven.'

(Matthew 5:13-16 THE MESSAGE)

08

RACHEL
aged 17

'I have a relative who isn't Christian and I've been praying for this person for a long time – for several years now. I prayed for this person to come to God and it was very frustrating.

All of a sudden she's started to go to church, and to pray and to talk about God openly. It's just amazing because I thought she would be the last person in the world to become a Christian. I mean, not the last person, but I thought it would be totally difficult for this person to accept Christ, and didn't know how it was going to happen, but it seems that right under my nose she's accepting Christ and that's an amazing prayer to have answered.'

REAL LIFE ST

OLLY ARENGO-JONES
aged 21, was a student at Oxford Brookes University

'I went to Oxford Brookes to study Economics and Accounting. When I arrived, church was the last thing on my mind.

I played rugby for the university and led a pretty wild life. The university rugby club is definitely a very non-Christian place to be.

You go out on Wednesday nights after the game and get absolutely wasted. The players go to a club in Cowley which is renowned (without being disrespectful) for having women who are not exactly virgins, if you know what I mean.

For most people at Brookes it is the best club and I thought it was great.

In fact, I was very happy with my life and could not complain at all.

My perception of Christians at the time was like a comedy sketch I saw where the Christians don't appear to have any muscles in their arms but just walk around with their hands flopping at their sides.

But then I met a guy called Will de Laszlo who was playing rugby with me. I met him half way through the first term and got on with him very, very well. I thought he was a fantastic guy, and somehow I got to know that he was a Christian.

He never came to the club on Wednesday nights until very late, when you would suddenly see him dancing. I later learned that he was doing an Alpha course. I just thought, 'This guy has different values to the rest of us.'

Then there was a girl at university called Katie – a fantastic girl – who was obviously different to every other girl.

There is a lot of bitchiness that hangs around a lot of girls, but Katie didn't have that. She too, I learned, was a Christian.

One Sunday Will invited me to church. I quite enjoyed it. The music was nice and the talk was good. I also met some of the church's student leaders and I met one guy called Matt and we talked about rugby for ages.

Then I started going out with Katie and I wasn't quite sure what I was getting into. I knew that we wouldn't be sleeping together or anything like that because of her Christianity and I was outwardly quite happy with that, but I wondered where it would go a few months down the line.

I thought to myself, 'How are you going to cope with this?'

I've only had two or three relationships in my life that have been serious and I never wanted to sleep with them immediately. It didn't seem right with those kind of relationships. So that's what I felt with Katie and I was quite OK with it.

I began to think more about Christianity. I had always believed there was a God and I never doubted that Jesus existed.

I did worry that if I did an Alpha course and became a Christian I would be doing it for Katie.

But I thought, 'Well, it's not going to work if I do it for her, is it? I've got to do it for me and my own faith.'

I read John's Gospel but when the

ORIES

September Alpha course came around, I thought, 'I'm not ready for this yet.'

In the end I did the April Alpha course. After months of putting it off, I said, 'Right, I'm going to do it' and I signed up.

As the course went on I got more and more agitated that no one had told me this stuff about Jesus before. Why didn't anybody at school teach me that?

On the Saturday afternoon of the weekend away my group leader and another member of the group prayed for me. As they prayed, I slowly started to cry – and then I found myself crying for ages.

I just felt so sorry for all the things I had done wrong. All the time I was thanking God for all that he had done for me – and every time I said 'thank you', I cried more. Every time I stopped crying I'd say 'thank you' again and start crying again.

We prayed for about half an hour and afterwards it was just amazing – genuine joy. It was the first time in my life I'd experienced such sheer joy.

By the end of the weekend, I found I was thinking about God all the time. He was constantly on my mind.

I wouldn't say that every action I've made since that weekend has been wholly Christian – I wouldn't say that at all – but every time I make a mistake the first thing I think about is God.

I'm still nowhere near a perfect Christian but I'm making progress.

Jesus is now in my mind the whole time and I make decisions based on my relationship with him and how I should be living my life from a Christian sense.

CONCLUSION*
Romans 1:16
**Never give up!
We might never know the effect of something that we have said or done, but God will use our lives and our words if we trust him.**

09

Does God Heal Today?

〉 ›〉〉〉 **_Introduction_**

The medical knowledge we have today is a gift from God. Alongside doing all that is medically correct, Christians pray and ask God to heal miraculously. Does God still heal today? Why should we expect him to?

HEALING IN THE BIBLE

Old Testament: God made promises that he would heal.

* 2 Kings 5
God said it was part of his character to heal.

There are examples of God healing.

New Testament: The example of Jesus – 25% of the Gospel stories are about Jesus healing.

* Matthew 9:35-10:8

The teaching of Jesus – he said healing was a sign of the Kingdom of God.

Jesus sent his disciples out to pray for healing.

Jesus also sends us out to heal in his name.

Jesus healed people because he loved them.
It is important that we care and want the best for anyone we pray for.

Prayers for healing should be simple, not long and complicated.

The Holy Spirit might guide us in how to pray:
✳with a picture in our minds.
✳with a sympathy pain.
✳with a strong feeling.
✳with words in our minds.
✳with words for us to speak.

When we pray we should:
ask: where it hurts, how long it has hurt, and why it hurts.

pray: that God would heal in the name of Jesus.

ask: that the Holy Spirit would heal the person.

continue: to be open to more guidance from the Holy Spirit.

Afterwards we should:
ask the person how they feel.

make sure that they are happy and understand all that has happened.

HEALING IN HISTORY
Acts 3:1-10
2

There have been examples of healing and miracles all through the history of the Christian church.

Primary Sources

'One day at three o' clock in the afternoon, Peter and John were on their way into the Temple for a prayer meeting. At the same time there was a man crippled from birth being carried up. Every day he was set down at the Temple gate, the one named Beautiful, to beg from those going into the Temple. When he saw Peter and John about to enter the Temple, he asked for a handout. Peter, with John at his side, looked him straight in the eye and said, "Look here." He looked up expecting to get something from them. Peter said, "I don't have a nickel to my name, but what I do have I give you: In the name of Jesus Christ of Nazareth, walk!" He grabbed him by the right hand and pulled him up. In an instant his feet and ankles became firm. He jumped to his feet and walked. The man went into the Temple with them, walking back and forth, dancing and praising God. Everybody there saw him walking around and praising God. They recognised him as the one who sat begging at the Temple's Gate Beautiful and rubbed their eyes, astonished, scarcely believing what they were seeing. The man threw his arms around Peter and John, ecstatic. All the people ran up to where they were at Solomon's Porch to see it for themselves.'

(Acts 3:1-10 THE MESSAGE)

'Science without religion is lame; religion without science is blind.'

Albert Einstein

When an old lady asked him the secret to his success, Alexander Fleming (the discoverer of Penicillin) replied: 'I can only suppose that God wanted Penicillin, and that was his reason for creating Alexander Fleming.'

DRESSINGS AND BANDAGES

FIRST-AID MATERIALS

The materials necessary for first-aid are usually kept together in a first-aid kit or some other suitable container. First-aid kits should be kept in the workplace, at sports and leisure facilities, in your home and car.

The contents of a kit for a workplace or leisure centre must conform to legal requirements; they should also

be clearly marked and readily accessible. The contents of the standard kit should form the your first-aid kit at home, alth you may wish to add to it.

Any first-aid kit must be ke dry atmosphere, and checked replenished regularly, so that th you need are always ready to

DRESSINGS

Fabric plaster / Waterproof plaster / Clear plaster / Heel and toe plaster

Adhesive dressings or plasters
Use for minor wounds. The waterproof types are the best choice for wounds on the hands.

Eye pad / Eye pad with headband

Sterile eye pads
Any injury to the eye needs the protection of a sterile covering.

Medium dressing / Large dressing / Extra-large dressing

Sterile dressings
These are easy to apply, so are ideal in an emergency. They come in a range of sizes, and a protective wrapping.

BANDAGES

Elastic and roller bandage / Conforming roller bandage / Crep roller bandage

Crepe roller bandage / Open-weave roller bandage

Roller bandages
Use these to give support to joints, secure d restrict movement, maintain pressure on a d or limit swelling.

Folded cloth triangular bandage / Folded pape triangular b

Triangular bandages
Made of cloth or strong paper, these can be u bandages and slings. If they are sterile and in wrapped, they may be used as dressings for l wounds and burns.

Tubular grip for limbs / Finger gauze

Tubular bandages
Use these specially shaped bandages for fing

AUTHORISED MANUAL

FIRST AID MANUAL

NEW FULLY PHOTOGRAPHIC 7th EDITION

Emergency procedures for everyone
at home, at work, or at leisure

c materials for a first-aid kit
ostly identifiable watertight box,
x adhesive dressings (plasters) in
ned sizes;
x medium sterile dressings;
vo large sterile dressings;
vo extra-large sterile dressings;
vo sterile eye pads;
x triangular bandages,
x safety pins;
sposable gloves.

• face shield;
• for outdoor activities: blanket, survival
bag, torch, and whistle.

HER USEFUL ITEMS

Safety pins

Clip

Pins and clips
Secure bandages or
dressings with these

Scissors and tweezers
Make sure scissors are
blunt-ended so that
they do not cause injury

Wound cleansing
wipes
Clean skin around
small wounds or your
hands with these, if
water and soap are

osable gloves
e gloves when
ting wounds or
ing of any waste
erials.

Tags
Use to label
of major acc

ase pads
is dressings, for extra
ding, or as swabs.

Plastic fac
This can pre
giving artifi

Conclusion
God does heal, but not every person and not every time.

☀**Doctors don't have a 100% success rate, but they don't stop being doctors and they don't stop trying.**

☀**If we never pray for anyone then nobody will ever be healed.**

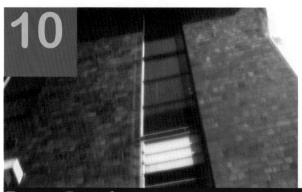

Introduction

People often think that the church is just a building.

People often think that the church is just for priests and nuns.

People often think that the church is just a service on Sundays.

People are often wrong.

So, what is the church all about?

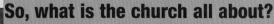

THE PEOPLE OF GOD

1 Peter 2:9-10

1

The church is not a building – it is made up of people.

The universal church includes all believers that have ever lived anywhere in the world at any time.

Today the church is huge – 1,900,000,000 people, more than 34% of the world's population.

Baptism is the visible mark of being a member of the church.

What about the church?

THE FAMILY OF GOD

1 John 4:19-5:1

2

God is our Father.
Jesus prayed that we would all be unified.
We are brothers and sisters and we relate to God and to one another in the church.

THE BODY OF CHRIST
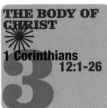
1 Corinthians 12:1-26

3

We are all one in the Holy Spirit, just as different parts make up one body.
We all have different gifts from God, just as different parts of the body have different roles.
We all need each other, just as the different body parts need each other.

A HOLY TEMPLE

Ephesians 2:19-22

4

A temple made of people – us.
Built on the foundation of the apostles and prophets in the New Testament.
With Jesus as the most important part – called the 'Cornerstone'.
The Holy Spirit lives in this special temple.

> 'Jesus Christ was fantastic, but I do not like the church. The church does more harm than good.'
> **Mick Jagger**

THE BRIDE OF CHRIST

Ephesians 5:25-27, 32

5

'It is so good to know that whatever country you can go to, you can worship the same God.'

Louise

Jesus loves his church like a groom loves his bride.

We, the church, should respond to Jesus by living holy lives, worshipping him, and telling others about him.

REAL LIFE STORIES

here is a saying about not being able to see the wood for the trees, I guess it means not getting the big picture (the wood) because the details (the trees) are right in your face, practically sticking up your nostrils. There should be a saying about not seeing the church for the church. I'd better elaborate ... Sometimes the biggest obstacle to seeing the majesty, importance and beauty of the church – in other words, to seeing the church as God sees it – is our experience of one particular church, the church we know best or even attend. However good our particular church is, it can't give us any

real concept of the universal church – of the wildly different ways and settings in which God is worshipped, and of the amazing diversity of people that love and serve him, and love and serve his people.

It says above that the universal church 'includes all believers that have ever lived anywhere in the world at any time'. That gives us two dimensions (space and time) to play with. At the present moment time travel is not an option (although the physicists tell us it's theoretically possible) but travel in the dimension of space is a real option. More and more Christian young people are

taking the opportunity to travel and to meet up with their peers in different churches. Some people travel down the street, others travel great distances to discover the church in far flung parts of the world. Either option is an excellent opportunity to get a far bigger idea of what the church is.

These comments, from European young people who travelled to South America (to take part in the 'Latino Experience' a short term mission trip arranged by the South American Mission Society), give some idea of the impact such a trip can have:

'It's been a challenge to me, and an encouragement – to get a sense of the global church, of the universal church. To see that the Lord is in every country of the world, that the church is in every country of the world.'

Daniel

'In Santa Cruz [Bolivia] we participated in a building project. It was supposed to be for four days, except I only managed the first day as I got bad food poisoning! I knew it was bad when I had two Bolivian women chattering to me in Spanish (I couldn't understand a word!) while bathing me with alcohol to get my fever down. My greatest memory of the trip is of those women who demonstrated such love and compassion to me when I was ill.'

Kate

Primary Sources

'We, though, are going to love – love and be loved. First we were loved, now we love. He loved us first.
If anyone boasts, "I love God," and goes right on hating his brother or sister, thinking nothing of it, he is a liar. If he won't love the person he can see, how can he love the God he can't see?
The command we have from Christ is blunt: Loving God includes loving people. You've got to love both.
Every person who believes that Jesus is, in fact, the Messiah, is God-begotten. If we love the one who conceived the child, we'll surely love the child who was conceived.'

(1 John 4:19-5:1 THE MESSAGE)

Conclusion

The church is about people: people in relationship with Jesus; people working together; people looking after one another; people serving and sharing good news with others.

'The welcome was just amazing compared to anything we'd have given them in England. I didn't understand a word of what was going on, but knew that the God they worshipped there was exactly the same God as I worship back in England.'

Susan

'Our experience in the Paraguayan Chaco was an unforgettable one, meeting such welcoming people who have so little, but who wanted to worship and pray with us. One particularly powerful moment was when we attempted to sing 'Thine Be the Glory' in their language Enxlet, which was difficult, but really showed how united we were despite the external differences between us. Their hospitality was such that they even barbecued a cow for us – tasty! The trip was an amazing experience, which taught me more about the universality of our faith and the awesome power of God. '

Hannah

talk4

Introduction Read: Romans 12:1–21

We get no mocks, trials or practice runs at life – so how can we be sure of making the most of it?

WHAT SHOULD WE DO?
Romans 12:2

1

Make a break with the past – don't be squeezed into the mould that makes you like everyone else.

Make a new start – let God transform you from the inside out.

We must make a decision to offer every part of our lives to God.

Our time – How do we use our time? How would God have us use it?

Our ambitions – Are our goals God's goals for us?

Our money – How do we use what we have? Selfishly or by giving?

How Can I Make the Most of the Rest of My Life?

Our ears – Do we choose to listen to gossip, or the best about others?

Our eyes – What do we choose to look at and watch – particularly on TV or in magazines?

Our mouth / tongue – The tongue is very powerful. What do we say?

Our hands – Do we give or do we take with our hands and skills?

Our sexuality – God has made us sexual and he knows how best it can be a pleasure to us.

Ourselves – God wants us to take off our masks.

We should recognise that if we live like this: others might laugh at us: there might be suffering and sacrifice.

talk4

REAL LIFE STORIES

The young career woman
Louisa

What do you do?

I work in London as an underwriter [insurer] for a Lloyd's Syndicate. At Lloyd's we insure all sorts of things, from ships to horses to lawyers. I work on an account that insures 'professional people' (such as lawyers, architects, engineers) for any mistakes that they may make in the course of their work – it's called Professional Liability.

What kind of skills / gifts do you have to have to do that?

I guess you need to be ok with numbers and you also need to be happy with negotiating – pretty much all the time. We take on people's risks – so you need to be able to do that and not lie awake at night worrying. You also need to be prepared to work mainly with men rather than women – women were only allowed into Lloyd's in the 1970s!

Does your work fit in with your general passions / goals for your life?

I was talking about this last night – I enjoy working in the city and I enjoy working with numbers.

Ultimately what motivates me is the chance to see people freed up from debt, or to see those that don't have much in life being given something by those that have. I really want to make a difference in this world. To me there is no point going to work day in day out just to take home a wage – it all seems rather meaningless.

I think it says somewhere in the Bible about being faithful with the small things in life so God can trust you with the bigger things. When I was a child there was a point at which I decided that I should tithe on my pocket money – I was just copying what the adults did. One day a friend of the family really needed money and so all my ten pences in a jar under my bed (which had built up to something quite substantial by then) were suddenly able to make a difference in someone's life. I really believe that God was laying foundations to motivate me to try and make a difference – to get money and materials out of the privileged city I work in and on to people who 'have not'.

How do you feel God helps you in the work situation?

I made a decision right at the beginning of my time in the city that I was going to be as truthful and transparent as I could be; to try and do things 'God's way'. I find that even in the hardest or most 'morally challenging' situations that if I strike out to maintain what my conscience tells me is correct then God backs me up or bails me out every time. As you do this more, so your faith grows and the next time becomes easier.

I am also a great believer in praying whenever situations look like they are going to get tough.

If I ask Jesus to go before me at work, then I trust that he will and those are the days when things tend to go a lot better. There is a lot to be said for nailing down a time with God each day – and it can be one of the hardest things to achieve. But, I find that the more I try and spend time with God, then the more solid and confident I feel about everything, not just work. I would like to think that the Holy Spirit is involved in every area of my life. That could range from making me a kinder person, to reminding me not to talk negatively about people, to guiding me in general decision making.

Finally ...

The worst thing would be to be left with the idea that I am some sort of extremely holy person who never puts a foot wrong. It is not a case of floating through life on a cloud. I make mistakes and let God down all the time, and that's an awful feeling. The best part is being able to talk to him and say 'help me get this right.'

talk4

Primary Sources

'So here's what I want you to do, God helping you: Take your everyday, ordinary life – your sleeping, eating going-to-work, and walking around life – and place it before God as an offering. Embracing what God does for you is the best thing you can do for him. Don't become so well adjusted to your culture that you fit into it without even thinking. Instead, fix your attention on God. You'll be changed from the inside out. Readily recognise what he wants from you, and quickly respond to it. Unlike the culture around you, always dragging you down to its level of immaturity, God brings the best out of you, develops well formed maturity in you.'

(Romans 12:1-2 THE MESSAGE)

'If a man hasn't found something he will die for, he isn't fit to live.

Martin Luther King

la

taste

new

hear

open

space

Conclusion

Why should we do it? Because God has a great plan for your future and this is the way to follow it. Because of all that God has done for us – we owe it to him

real

spirit

la

intuitive

"I wear my shadows where they're harder to see but they follow me everywhere... i guess that should tell me I'm travelling toward light, I guess something you sang made me remember that... I guess I'm sayin' thanks for that"

Bruce Cockburn

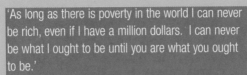

'As long as there is poverty in the world I can never be rich, even if I have a million dollars. I can never be what I ought to be until you are what you ought to be.'

Martin Luther King

'All you need is love'

Lennon and McCartney